Life's
Poetic
Dichotomies

Books by the Anonymous Author and Artist

Her Poetic Rise

It is for the religiously poetic that blends religion and feminism.

Life's Short Stories

Fictional characters vie to live their own lives.

Life's Mixed Poetry

Poems are mixed schematically, stylistically, and randomly.

Life's Novellas: Fate Waits Upon No One

The good and the bad are juxtaposed, chronologically, fictionally, and theatrically.

Their Poetic Minds

Poems are juxtaposed, religiously, femininely, and dichotomously.

Poems of Life

Poems are mixed schematically, stylistically, and randomly.

Life's Heart Break: A Novella

In the end, will Zenald discover what may be one of life's biggest heart-breaks: heart-ache?

Duty & Destruction I

A real female experiences life in and out of the U.S. military.

Art Book

The Diamond & Heart Art Collections

Pictures are exhibited, categorically, by coloring schemes and coloring mediums; all of which, have been affected with special effects.

Schemes: pastel shades; earth tones; primary colors; gray, black and white; black and white.

Mediums: colored pencils; water coloring; pastel coloring; acrylic coloring; oil coloring.

Life's Poetic Dichotomies

Anonymous

Century Conquests

Life's Poetic Dichotomies

Copyright © 2009 by Anonymous

www.centuryconquests.com
info@centuryconquests.com

ISBN: 978-0-9850698-1-0

First printing: Fall 2009

Century Conquests' rev. date. 09/01/10

Cover graphic designed by: Century Conquests © 2013

Century Conquests ® 2012

Life's Poetic Dichotomies

Anonymous

Acknowledgements

For the small voice deep inside me that wants me to carry on poetically.

I thank those, too, who have helped with the publication of this book.

I also thank each and every reader of my book for permitting me the privilege, to exhilarate, and enchant, and even enlighten you.

Author's Note

Withstanding its extended products or services or even the lack there of, this book was published, previously, by a so-called "Subsidy Publisher, or Vanity Publisher"; whose cover design and interior both were different than this book's.

This book has been redesigned, revised, and republished—since, under the direction of a brand new entity.

A Self Accuser

Your mistress, that you follow whores, still taxeth you:
'Tis strange she should confess it, though it be true.

—John Donne
(1572-1631)

Introduction

Life has its dichotomies.

How is man or woman supposed to be very obedient while so desiring his or her Creator's forbidden fruit? I have almost always been attracted to, and repelled by some of life's biggest dichotomies: like, hope and despair; faith and doubt; ambition and sloth; strength and weakness—or, ups and downs: peace and pother; health and sickness; love and heartache; happiness and sadness; success and failure—or, even, gains and losses: lightness and darkness; prettiness and ugliness; rightness and wrongness; plus, goodness and badness—or, joy and sorrow, and so forth.

It is, so ironically, such dichotomies of life that three of life's greatest minds and bodies so struggled with here on Earth some 365, plus, years—ago. (Even so, we should also know that such still exists....) I am referring to the Medieval philosopher—or, Saint Augustine (354-430); the Renaissance spiritualist—or, Aemilia Lanyer (1569-1645); and even, the Jacobean meta-physician—or, John Donne (1572-1631); all of whom struggles were almost, certainly, complicated, right, by what seemingly mattered most during their very eras: religion, or the lack thereof.

Not very surprising, either, was that religion and what it went against often-times rested, and restlessly, right, at the core of their personal and professional struggles. Saint Augustine sought constantly to just integrate his un-spiritual self with his spiritual self. Aemilia Lanyer sought constantly to just elevate her Feminine self with the use of her spiritual self far above all else. That oppressed her and even other Females. John Donne sought constantly to just integrate his in-corporeal self with his corporeal self. Yet, it has been John Donne's dichotomous struggle that interest me the most.

Or, rather, there is no better place that we will find in time, one's mind, heart, and body, and even soul quite against—that; which breathes life right into the same soul, body, and heart, and even mind. Or, more, to the point, what, how, when, and where, and even why such struggle can and does affect one's ethics, morality, and character—or life; which gives voice to the poetic speaker advocating for, or advocating against, or even abstaining: right, in the midst of some dichotomous struggle.

More, it is in the middle or even underneath experiencing such struggles; or such dichotomies of life that certain forces or powers just come right into play, in particular, gender. The mental, emotional, physical, spiritual, and the like—or, influences, which influence life and even one, so personally, warrant some exploration, as well. Ethics and its ability, too, to effectuate certain moral principles must be included, some-what, in the mix of such powers or forces: or, even, influences—or better, in the dichotomies of life.

Such has everything to do with the rightness and wrongness of one's actions; plus, the goodness and badness of the motives and ends of such actions. It is of great import, what motivates one toward some motive or a specific motive. For, it often-times dictates a certain behavior pattern that just accompanies a certain face: like, a male, or a female, who exhibits one identity, on one occasion; then, on another occasion, exhibits an entirely different identity, or face. For what reason does he or she does so; and, to what actual avail?

There exists some ambivalence in such scenario, moreover, yet it is not enough to keep it from happening. The bitter-sweet irony is also that such ambiguity serves only as a source of frustration. That just gnaws at the core of his or her being: A being that is just caught or trapped, inevitably, right, in an inevitable imbroglio. Plus, it is utterly unable to free it-self right from the perilous integrity of its conduct. This, largely, was what so boggled John Donne throughout his entire life-time: His trying yet quite often in vain, to obtain, and retain, and even maintain that very delicate balance of true-ness; to some higher principles other than his very own self-imposed principles of life and its resultant methodologies.

But, as we all can and must agree and—right, along, with John Donne; that such efforts to be free from indistinctness or, a see-sawing of sort—fall way short, quite often. This zig-zagging, or even double-sidedness—as it were, almost, always, leads straight to being double-tongued, and double-acting, (or, even, wig-wagging); with-standing some double-standard with respect to sex, (or something else, in nature). Then, there are the other influences: religious, social, and so on; by their very nature, which affects one's mind, heart, and body, and even spirit, morally.

Furthermore, morality, and its ability to alter behavior; whose conduct could be either right or wrong and motives good or bad is of some essence. Acknowledging that a certain measure of double-minded-ness exists so in-evitably in the double-faced person's life; because, of one influence or another influence, what must we presume, or assume, next? Bearing right in mind what the struggle is all about: double-dealing mind-ful-ness. How, then, does such struggle further affect one's conduct be it either right or wrong and motives either good or bad?

Most likely, one's behavior and the motive that brings about and then reinforces such behavior, so centers around the dichotomies of life; and, whether one is under some cover; or inside of some haven; or outside of it: at home, at work, at church, at court, at play, and the like; hence, the physical, mental, religious, spiritual, social, political, and, emotional, and even more, influences. That affect one doubly and even one's gender—or being, life: while at play; while at court; while at church; while at work; while at home, and so forth.

In addition, and, in any case, such influences almost always converge upon the two greatest dichotomies of life: the un-spiritual, and the spiritual; both of which, once, again, so confounded, if not ate away at the very crux of Saint Augustine's; and, Aemilia Lanyer's; and even, John Donne's foundation(s) of life: Such just affected their minds, hearts, and bodies, and even spirits, most profoundly.

Yet, no one, and, quite certainly, no poet, in my very strong opinion, has since articulated the heavy burden on, and the heavy unburdening of, the dichotomous double-sidedness; as seen in one's person more so than Donne: or, the masterful meta-physician. He has so captured, rather single-handedly, the ultimate nature of existence, reality, and experience: albeit, in super self-contained, plus super self-conceptual systems; that, not surprising, is seen in his poetry, so particularly, in his clever conceits. This comparison, usually, right, in verse—couplets, between seemingly different objects are them-selves the embodiment of the dichotomy: or, double-mindedness, or even, double-sidedness.

Further, we now know what some of the great big dichotomies of life are; plus, how they affect one and when and even where such double-sidedness occurs. But, I have yet to address why such dichotomies transpire, until now. For, it may very well be of the greatest import, so affecting conduct. More precisely, one's motives—or, why he or she chooses to show one identity vice another identity or even some other identity. Or, put forth a certain face on some certain occasion vice some other occasion or even another occasion. In the end, such shows some character.

Or, even, such speaks right to the mind-set of the double-dealing male or female. And, more often than not, he or she is just seeking some sort of fulfillment: emotional, political, social, spiritual, religious, mental, or physical, or even something else..., in nature; all of which, just, converge, eventually. The convergence of such motivation— or, influences, can and does cause one's dual faces and even double-sided behavior. That only adds to the aggregate qualities of his or her personality, or, character.

Finally, the mix of such dichotomous traits serves—only, to complicate matters, or one's life, or even being, character. Keeping up certain appearances, at some certain place and/or time vice some other place and/or time, does not come so easily; especially, to those who claim to be, almost, always, right, and good. The problem almost certainly being that he or she has to, at some point, or another point, in time, advocate for, or just advocate against, or even abstain right in the middle of living his or her life: right, to the fullest extent, with-standing its ups and downs. Or, highs and lows that precipitate and then perpetuate double forms of behavior in dealing with such ups and downs: whether at home, or out in town, or even elsewhere.

It is, too, in the spirit of double-mindedness; or, how, what is real and what is false in the written or practical code of one's conduct; that, I have explored, poetically, and religiously, and even secularly: Being righteously good on one occasion. Then, on another occasion, or even some other occasion, being quite the opposite, wrongfully bad, and so on. Thus, such exploration is explored, as well—and, just, as I have said, since, right, from none other than the dichotomously poetic view-point of John Donne: or, the marvelously masterful meta-physician.

A Would-Be Winner

You really want to win, especially, in the end:
Yet, you're first scar'd to lose—quite possibly, because of your damnably dark sin.

A.

Part I

An Optimist

In life, she's almost always sought to collar Hope,

Only, to find out in the end—that, it can't ev'r be fully yoked or roped.

A Pessimist

Because of her hopelessness, she just goes on mir'd by Despair:

Like a great big female grizzly bear, that cares nothing for being the wild's would-be

heir.

A Dreamer

To make his fate come true, he has such hope, ambition, and strength, and even some patience, but lacks Faith.

Yet, he just persists in the utterly un-merciful face of delay;

Since, the fulfillment of his destiny has almost always made him wait.

Faithful

Being un-filled, his lot in life remains, roundly, in Doubt,
Withstanding its total tout, it still amounts to nil—or zip;
None of which, will stop the faith-less man from being undoubtedly devout.

Girl Power

At work, the gang of gals possesses some Ambition.

      Still, they're mir'd by their femininity;

            It sometimes causes their indecision;

Thereby leaving them with noticeable gullibility—or, vulnerability.

Secret Slackers

At home, the men are little more than Sloths;

     For this, their women would give a great big vouch.

While out and about, others see them as extremely energetic men on the move;

     When they're on the move, they ev'n have to be soothed.

Muscles

In God's word, the female finds Strength,

Grabbing hold of it whilst it's slipping right away;

Because, the force of His word almost nev'r widens the width,

Widening down and then contracting around, at the end of the day;

Thus, her staying power just continues shrinking back to its original length.

The Underbelly

In the Devil's world, the male wrestles with Weakness,

   While his ethics, morality, and character all sink into a state of nakedly dark sin;

His darkly diabolical behavior, just the same, is almost nev'r seamless,

   While at the same time, the male wishes to be on some roundly righteous mend;

Yet, he just goes on perfecting it (weakness) with such keenness.

Part II

Giving One's Word

Early on, the lady learn'd the value of Commitment;

But, if any agreement prov'd—later, to have been in-opportune, she simply broke such

Covenant.

Double-Dealer

At church, the gentle man swears off the biggest sort of Infidelity;

When he's not at church, howev'r, he indulges whole-heartedly in perfidy or,

Treachery.

Backbone

In the end, the female wins only because of her Perseverance.

Yet, in the beginning, her persistence wins over nothing on Earth.

She, still, un-earths the lasting quality that's always necessary to bear anything—

Endurance.

Throwing in the Towel

Being so tir'd of see-sawing, or zig-zagging, or even damn wig-wagging,

I'm finally calling it Quits;

But, not, before turning around, ambivalently, and witlessly, all over again.

Because, my wits have since done more than just limp'd off a bit.

Iron-Heartedness

It's what propels the female civilian to become a female sailor—Courage,

    Doing so, unfortunately, without realizing such: its full ramifications.

Still, the sailor has nev'r thought—once, that her tour of duty would be an easy

    Voyage;

    But, just, like most things that ultimately rear their real colors, or content,

    This civilian-sailor now has some circularly colorful complications.

Afraid of One's Shadow

Born and bred, at home, to be something far more than a nakedly weak Coward;

It's just that such future seems rather sour as, to make her glower and then cower.

The girl is looking—still, to her beautifully bright future yet is afraid to face it down;

And, she's bound or taken down—in-arguably, like some weakly naked clown.

Part III

Cease-Fire

Because the boy can't have it at home, he instead seeks it while at school, Peace.

If his parents were to just cease their fuss and feather—then, he'll find, quite possibly, a brand new lease;

On his young life with some measure of ease, for this is no tease.

Tempest in a Teapot

At court, she's a colorfully and a circularly choky cloud that's pretty full of physical
Pother;

On, the other hand, when there's no up-standing man around, she dares not to bother.

Tip-Top Shape

I've almost always exercis'd to better my Health;

    When all has been done—or exercis'd—then, what's left, death?

Throw-Ups

His education, training, and experience, could or would nev'r be enough,

To keep it away, Sickness;

Heedless, the doctor remains quite ignorant of his own starkly or darkly if not

Deathly diagnosis;

Even as the roundly rotten growth growing inside his body grows with such

Rottenness.

One's All

I'll find it on a circularly and a colorfully rainy yet sunny or lovely day—Love:
Like the beautifully white-colored bird, that roundly represents peace, purity,
      And gentleness—dove.
    Then, on the next day, it'll fly far away:
    Like, a big black cloud leaving behind a darkly un-lovable day that's no longer
      At bay. HOORAY!

Heartbreak

The woman has begun to hate the man that's caused her such Heartache;

His love has prov'n to be fake yet somehow real but still shaky and fated.

This being why she, almost, always, feels, as if theirs is an in-escapable relationship of

A rape:

It's a not so dated or under-rated but jaded relation that should've been long ago,

Vacated.

Creature Comforts

The man almost nev'r wants it when it's available, Pleasure.

Signing, often-times, in dis-pleasure at the mere thought of it being given freely to him;

He instead steals it—pleasure, when it's un-available, howev'r, gradual.

Because, it's almost always about some super big win:

Or, the starkly dark thrill of the small steal that gives him the most

Rapture.

Crown of Thorns

At work, the females endure some Pain;

It's because of their co-workers' (or the males') efforts to just keep them faceless.

It's a small price, just the same, to pay for their big gains,

Although the females will still appear aimless;

Never again, though, will their winnings just wane or be maim'd, in vain!

Paradise

When he's not with the woman, the man feels such Happiness;

When she feels him, he becomes mask-less;

When the woman's with the man, he feels such sadness;

When she feels him, it's by no means pain-less;

When he's not with the woman, the man just savors all the madness.

Bleeding Heart

When she's with the man, the woman feels such gladness;

    When he touches her, she becomes name-less;

When the man's with the woman, she feels such Unhappiness;

    When he touches her, it's by no means ache-less;

When she's not with the man, the woman just flavors all the insaneness.

Master Stroke

Without doubt or fail, the female executive earns her Success.

Yet, she sometimes thinks that it's all in vain:

Journeying back and forth and all around from north to south and east to west;

It's been a long, hard, and painful, yet successful journey—or, big gain.

That others believed she'd nev'r obtain, attain.

Plus, the nakedly nominal nay-sayers ev'n think that she's only out to impress.

But, they can nev'r know the female executive's actual aim.

Checkmate

At work, you almost always try to avoid any kind of Failure.

As the company's higher-ups will hold you undoubtedly responsible and accountable;

For, the type of responsibility and accountability of your job allows for no blunder or,

Error.

If some sort of error or blunder should occur—then, you're not necessarily gone.

As such higher-ups, still, will hold you undoubtedly responsible and accountable;

For, the kind of responsibility and accountability of your job doesn't allow for another

clone—or, another damned drone.

Step Forward

We now can take a little rest because of our super big Gain.

Just, the same, that we can't afford to let such respite take a bite out of our progress;

For it's caus'd us such un-due pain.

However, we still must endure it (pang); otherwise, we stand to digress or regress:

Way, back, to a time when our lives are liv'd in a high, and wide, and even darkly, if not, a nakedly painful chain.

Just the same—that, we can still afford to take a little rest because of our advancement;

This, by the way, on some bright or gray or ev'n dark day, will cause us to feel definite detachment.

Dead Loss

Take what you want or need from life, keeping in mind that it has a cost;

      Whose price may very well be a great big Loss:

A price so damn high that it'll hammer you right down,

      Begging to give back—that, which you've thus taken from life—POUND!

On the ground, being pounded around, won't be nearly enough, howev'r,

        For life to stop such pounding or exacting payment;

      As it'll only be the start-up fee for your bereavement:

An encroachment of sort, by which you take what you need or want from life;

      Such may very well be too goddamn high of a cost—or, price.

Light-Heartedness

At church, the girl feels such Joy,

        Feeling God's words soundly saturate her soul;

Its core once oppressively coy—but, no more; for it's now bold,

             Feeling His wonderful words propel her soul to soar.

             At church, still, the girl wants to roar,

                  Feeling God's un-wonderful words oppress her spirit;

        Its core once quite full of joy—but, no more; for it's now a dark mirror,

Seeing it toy with her spirit: that's just mirroring a damnably black boy.

Millstone Round One's Neck

It's almost always about my joy and Sorrow,

    Whether I've too much of one and not enough of the other;

In either case, it's almost certain that both will be right with me tomorrow.

    It's, also, the latter—sorrow—whose substance just sweetens my pother.

Is it possible to have too much of one and not enough of the other?

    In either case, it's almost certain that both will leave me in a few days.

      It's, also, the former—joy—whose content just causes me to holler!

      Again, it's almost always about my joy and sorrow;

Both of which live in the black-blue yonder—yet, visit me daily in many ways.

Part IV

Glare

It's what shines upon the man in his darkest hour of need, Lightness;
Yet, he's un-able to see it because he's blind to the evil ways of woman-kind, sightless.

Witching Hour

It's what lights up the woman's life, striking Darkness.

  But, she's still able to see what's light—or right.

Since, it (blackness) doesn't just fade away leaving her without a scratch, mark-less.

Pretty as a Picture

At court, the female relies on it to make her day, Prettiness.

More, to ensnare her male prey, she ev'n doles out an extra dose of wittiness.

Just, the same, that her all is nev'r enough to keep such prey;

Because, he always slips away, wanting not to experience any morally wrong decay.

Hard-Favored

At work, the male manager's managerial style is that of Ugliness;

    He just wants to maintain a certain level of meanness.

At home, though, his managerial style is that of loveliness;

    For his lovely wife simply can't and won't tolerate any unseemliness.

    Plus, such, almost, always, accounts for the manager's leanness.

Fair and Square

At church, the worshiper's words and actions both are about Rightness.

He rises up in prayer whilst his dark soul just floats down to the Monarch of Hell.

When he leaves it—church, the man feels such mightiness;

The might ev'n propels him to yell; then, it delivers the man from a down-right dim jail:

Or, an evil cell.

He plans, as well, to tell anyone that'll listen—that,

Nothing in God's world could or would ev'r cause him to fail:

Not ev'n his heavy, wide, and diabolically black tail.

Off Target

Because of the woman's brilliancy, there's nev'r any room for Wrongness.

She's right, too, to keep up the damn fight when others try to wrong her.

Just the same, that her brilliance is what almost always causes her loneness.

If she'd just accept some man's roundly romantic dare;

Then, there'll be quite possibly a right and a wrong—or,

A romantically un-ev'n pair.

Since the woman could or would nev'r consider lessening her rightness;

As such, stance is only fair:

Lest she just wants to end up quite sightless.

Honest-to-Goodness

At church, the pastor preaches Goodness,

    For it gives him a real sense of fullness.

At work, he takes further pride in what's good;

    It's easy to do so; because, he, almost, always, wears a didactically righteous

                      Hood.

At court, however, all that's good undermines the very validity of his morality or piety;

    It's the kind of good, that's not hood'd with integrity or purity.

At church, once again, the pastor is un-able to preach.

    It's because of his impurity and immorality while at play—or, court,

circularly—and, rather colorfully.

Black-Hearted

At play, the class of men almost certainly is oblivious of their

Badness;

Living their lives both haphazardly and promiscuously:

It leaves them, in the end, so full of sadness.

In the suspicious eyes of their women, such is seen and felt most conspicuously;

Living their lives with weak and foolish men:

It leaves them, the women, in the end, quite mad and sad, obviously.

In the blind eyes of their men, they again can't and won't see their own dark sins;

Living their lives as starkly if not darkly foolish and weak men, sinners:

It leaves them un-able to bend—or win, and then be on the mend—in the end.

Level-Headed

The old man is grateful for his Saneness,

Although it isn't nearly enough to keep him going;

Yet, it somehow keeps him from waning and becoming nameless.

Secretly, howev'r, it's still hard doing his towing and sowing.

The same old man is ev'n un-grateful, some-times, for his soundness;

It's just enough to keep him going.

And others view this as a man whose life is that of roundness.

Still, the man finds none of it soothing;

Since his sanity is almost always here today and then long gone by tomorrow.

It's quite simply the relationship between his inescapably dark joy and

His super sour sorrow.

Not Quite Right

The young woman is well aware of her Madness.

   For it's enough to keep her coming and going;

It ev'n gives her a measure of gladness.

   That, she often-times likes doing such crazy sowing.

For, the young woman feels as if she's in another world—or, the real world;

   It's in the depths of such darkly deranged world—again, where she likes towing.

Yet, what the woman doesn't know is that her world is really a dark, deep, and

   Dangerous hell.

   Though, it's still where she's most at home, alone.

It all just makes the young woman want to yell; she may very well not live to tell—that,

   Nothing in her world of a cell or a jail has ev'r been well!

Just, the same, that the young woman dare not dream of ev'r leaving her place of abode;

   Since, it's taken hold of her like wide, thick, and black mold.

   It dares not dream of ev'r letting the young woman go—OH NO!

Tide of Events

The dark pair of lovers both loath and love living their Life;

For their lives has been quite a lovely match.

Yet, their love almost, always, causes one of them to take to a butcher's knife.

Still, the female lover has been some catch.

Her lot in life dictates such;

The lovers travel down a roundly rocky road.

Just the same, that the male lover believes—that, the toll-road—or rock isn't much;

For, the female lover, almost, certainly, lightens their real load.

Plus, the lovers' darkly loveless love just adds to the madness inside their gladness.

Still, it's a lovely life that's based on being marvelously mis-match'd;

Their un-lovable lot in life dictates such a mix of goodness and badness.

In fact, the pair of lovers' un-lovely match—or, love, has only just begun to hatch.

Again, the dark twosome both loath and love, truly, living their lives;

They just love each other while stab one another brutally with jagged butchers' knives.

The Great Adventure

Quite full of life, the wealthy haves are almost ready for its ending—Death.

Should the wealthy also care about their damnably dying fame?

Needless to say, that they're rather reluctant to leave behind their wealth;

Since its acquisition has caused them such damn pain.

Yes, indeed, the haves have been badly maimed.

Fortunately, though, such sweetly sour pang is lessened by their power;

It's the type of power that's almost always needed for them to be tamed:

Be so just like a poisonously black flower.

And, it dares not holler…!

Being so near death, the dark flowers—or, haves, could sure use another hour to flower their fantastically fallible fates.

It'll be time used not for prayer but instead to just wallow;

They'll bother to indulge their hates, having transpired on certain dates, and, with certain or utterly un-celestial mates.

Quite full of life, the wealthy have-nots are now ready for its ending—hell;

It's only another place of abode where they'll live deliberately well.

That's like a dark, deep, and dirty, and even dangerous, yet delicious jail of a cell.

Conclusion

Again, life has its dichotomies.

In the spirit of double-mindedness, does his or her double-minded behavior just so happen because of some practical or even written code concerning one's dichotomous conduct; which can be either real or fake? Being genuine on one occasion, and then on another occasion, or even some other occasion, being very different, so counterfeit. Yet, again, the complication almost certainly being that he or she at some point in time, or another time, has to just switch internal or external or even ulterior roles: or, behavior patterns—motives, which eventually complicate matters or one's life—being, character: in right or wrong ways—and, in good or bad ways, and so forth.

I have showed such, even, via the use of various kinds of rhymes: masculine—complain/disdain; and, feminine—fortunate/importunate; and, even, slant—years/yours; plus, sometimes, perfect—brain/chain; rhyme schemes—aa, aba, abab, ababa, and so on; plus, types of poems—couplets—aa, bb, cc, dd...; terza rimas—aba, bcb, cdc, ded...; quatrains—abab, cdcd, efef, ghgh...; whose very variation in stanzas—(or even lines), in conjunction with the various rhyme schemes comprises, to some extent, variant sonnets: Shakespearean—abab, cdcd, efef, gg; Petrarchan (Italian)—abbaabba, cdecde; plus, Spenserian—abab, bcbc, cdcd, ee. A sonnet is so typically 14 lines of poetry. Using the above poetic devices, the poems have since taken on a set form, or a regular form vice an irregular form, or an un-set form: the former being like a sonnet; and, the latter being just like free verse. I have shown, further, in the varied poems such dichotomies of life as seen in the poetic characters' lives. It all brings about and then reinforces the double-sidedness in one's conduct because of one influence or another influence.

Furthermore, his or her personality—or even character is so influenced—or even pre-disposed, ultimately. Because, of such duality while having so sought some sort of fulfillment: mental, emotional, physical, religious, spiritual, social, or political, or even something else, in nature. One's frame of mind has been altered in one way or another way for one reason or another reason. Hence, him or her having so chosen to show one identity versus another identity or even some other identity; or, putting forth a certain face on a certain occasion, at the end of the day, exhibits some character.

And, most, if not all of the poetic characters that I have constructed in the poems through out this poetry book, personify, if not exemplify, this notion of changing faces: or, identities—personas. They do such, most interestingly, at both very opportune and very in-opportune times. Or, times that almost always suit their fancies if not wants or needs. Obviously, such poetic characters have some motives be they good or bad, whose actions can be either right or wrong. It is almost, always, that we will see such motives put right into action; whose motivations—or, actions, are enacted at home, work, church, court, or play, or even else where, respectively: like, for example, in the poems, "Secret Slackers," and "Girl Power," and even "The Underbelly."

Additionally, I have constructed most if not all of the poems in this poetry book with an emphasis on that; which is often seen in the meta-physician's, or John Donne's poetry—conceits: Or, comparisons between essentially different things or notions, un-paralleled imagery, and manipulation of words; which brings to life, so eventually, those images or dichotomous representations. Once, more, it was what gnawed right at the gist of Donne's struggle, or his life—being.

This heavy burden on, and heavy un-burdening of one's dichotomous double-minded-ness; or, double-sided-ness in an effort to obtain, and retain, and even maintain, yet often-times, right, in vain, that fragile balance of being honest; to some other higher standards than one's own self-imposed standards of life and its methodological rules, or reasoning. Withstanding life's great big dichotomies or its highs and lows or even its ups and downs—or, gains and losses, and the like; none are as relevant as the two biggest dichotomies of all: spiritual, and un-spiritual. These, two, great big dichotomies of life are seen, so very vividly, for instance, in the poems: "A Dreamer"; "Faithful"; "Creature Comforts."

More, the two biggest dichotomies of life, or corporeal and in-corporeal, plus their dichotomous affect upon him or her maybe seen keenly while one is in or out: or, at home, at work, at church, at court, at play, and so forth, with-standing other influences: mental, emotional, physical, religious, spiritual, social, or, political, or, even, something else, such as, gender. Such, almost, certainly, precipitates, and then perpetuates his or her double-minded behavior either right or wrong and motives either good or bad.

We see this duplicitous conduct, too, in the various poems that I have constructed all through this poetry book. How his or her behavior is one way on one occasion, and then different on some other occasion, or even different on another occasion: "Double-Dealer," and "Tempest in a Teapot," and so on. What is more, is how one's dichotomous conduct is stepped up some, in time, or stepped down some, in time, with regard to sex. That, some female may very well want or need to use her feminine wiles—more so, than her male counterpart's need or want to use his masculine wiles. Where such happens is even more interesting, happening, say, at court, instead of, at church.

In addition, two particular influences, religious and social, influenced greatly not only John Donne's mind, heart, and, body, and, even, soul; but, also, such influenced greatly Aemilia Lanyer's..., and even Saint Augustine's..., still. Re-calling what often-times went right against their personal and professional struggles in life, religion, and its social consequences. Inescapably, such social ramifications headed straight to morality. What was morally good or bad and right or wrong? Perhaps, it was nothing more or less than the obvious and the very duplicitous dichotomy, it-self: good, bad, and right, and even wrong; all, eating right off each other while at the same time fending right off one another.

With-standing what-ever double-standard (with respect to gender), double-acting behavior, and double-talking—or double-sided-ness; this zig-zagging—or, see-sawing—or, even, wig-wagging of sort, did not free him or her from the haphazardly hazardous honesty of one's conduct. Just the same, that they—or, Saint Augustine, Aemilia Lanyer, and John Donne, all tried to strike some balance of trueness; to some higher power other than their own power; and, even, to transpose such higher power onto their own lives, or beings. Such is seen, as well, right, in the very different poems all over this poetry book: "Muscles," and "Backbone," and the like.

Moreover, it is in or even in between experiencing such; aspiring, absolutely, to a far greater principle, (or the lack there of), other than one's own self-imposed principles of life, and methods of living it, life; which ultimately brings into play his or her actions, or one's conduct: whether such behavior is either ethical or not, or, either right or wrong; plus, whether the ends of such actions are either good or bad. What is the real motivation behind his or her conduct, we should ask. Such motivation also almost always dictates one's behavior and even more, depending on the circumstance or the occasion: whether he or she is at work, at home, at church, at court, at play, and so forth.

This big transformation or changing of identities on one occasion versus another occasion or even some other occasion, as it were, is seen keenly in the poems all through this poetry book. It is where poetic characters, like, in the poems, "Iron-Heartedness," and "Master-Stroke," and such, seek, rather seriously, to up-grade them-selves: whether mentally, emotionally, physically, religiously, spiritually, socially, or politically, or even otherwise. Yet, at the same time, they just down-grade them-selves by their dichotomous actions: Exhibiting various identities—or, faces, on various occasions—that, once more, almost, always, suit their purposes or fancies.

It is not surprising, either, how this dichotomous behavior can and often does brings about and then reinforces such struggle. It is a conflict, which often rests, very restlessly, right, at the crux of his or her personal and professional struggles. Yet, again, it rested roundly at the core of Saint Augustine's struggles, Aemilia Lanyer's struggles, and, especially, John Donne's struggles: How they sought, constantly, to integrate their two selves, spiritual and un-spiritual, and, sometimes, three selves, in the case of Lanyer: feminine, and spiritual, and even un-spiritual. However, it is John Donne's, or the meta-physician's struggle that has so interested me. There has been no better place in time for us to travel to—but, to a tiny window of John Donne's pretty poetic mind.

We have seen, so subsequently, looking right through it—a tiny yet most mindful window, how one's soul, body, and heart, and even mind can be quite against that; which so breathes life right into the same mind, heart, and body, and even soul. Or, most pointedly, we have come to know through this book's poems and poetic characters, what some of life's biggest dichotomies are; plus, how, when, where, and, even, why they some-times transpire. Or rather, we have seen through such poems and poetic characters, the affect, if not effect—that, ethics, morality, and character have on one, one's life, or being. It just gives voice to the poetic speaker or character advocating for, advocating against, or abstaining—right, in the middle of some dichotomous struggle.

Lastly, how is man or woman supposed to be obedient while definitely desiring his or her Creator's forbidden fruit? Is it because he or she is so simply and inescapably attracted to, and repelled by it—forbidden fruit, so simultaneously? Or, quite probably, it is nothing more or less than the dichotomy of life, it-self: Its ups, downs, gains, losses, and, joys, and, even, sorrows; that just can not help—but, to chew right off each other, while at the same time, to spew right out one another: like, hope and despair; faith and doubt; ambition and sloth; strength and weakness; peace and pother; health and sickness;

love and heartache; happiness and sadness; success and failure; lightness and darkness; prettiness and ugliness; rightness and wrongness; plus, goodness and badness—or, joy and sorrow. Once again, such are some of the big dichotomies of life. That three of life's greatest minds and bodies struggled with here on Earth some 365, plus, years, ago: The Medieval philosopher—Saint Augustine; the Renaissance spiritualist—Aemilia Lanyer; plus, the Jacobean meta-physician—John Donne.

They all sought, and simply, to integrate their corporeal and in-corporeal selves. Granted, such integration was not easy, at all. Since, it was difficult, at best, or worst, so impossible, possibly, to do such, in actuality, because of their absolute afflictions. Even in today's world, it can be very hard trying to integrate the religious and the secular: that which is repressed or oppressed, and that which is liberated. Thus, is it any big wonder that he or she assumes some identity; or, even, exhibits a certain face on some certain occasion, or another certain occasion, or even some other certain occasion; to lessen his or her repression or oppression; or, to just increase his or her liberation; and, to do so— right, in the midst of life's ups and downs—or, gains and losses? In the end, I am so obligated to just say it: That, it is just how the awfully bitter-sweet cup-cake of life, in due course, so crumbles, and, quite, conversely. One's joys finally feed right off one's sorrows and vice versa.

Reference

Smith, A.J.; Tobin, John. *John Donne. The Complete English Poems*. London: The Penguin Group, Inc., 1996.